The best mates guide to

# Bedroom-blitzing and other room revamps

★ Gill Sutherland ★

Scholastic Children's Books
Commonwealth House, 1–19 New Oxford Street,
London, WC1A 1NU, UK
A division of Scholastic Ltd
London ~ New York ~ Toronto ~ Sydney ~ Auckland
Mexico City ~ New Delhi ~ Hong Kong

Published in the UK by Scholastic Ltd, 2003
Text copyright © Gill Sutherland, 2003
Illustrations copyright © Kirstie Aitken, 2003

ISBN 0 439 97827 0

Printed and bound by Nørhaven Paperback A/S, Denmark

2 4 6 8 10 9 7 5 3 1

The right of Gill Sutherland and Kirstie Aitken to be identified as the author
and illustrator of this work respectively has been asserted
by them in accordance with the Copyright, Designs and
Patents Act, 1988.

# Contents

# ✯ Want to be Mates? ✯

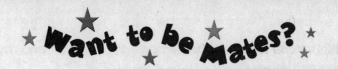

The name's Molly, Molly White. (Bit dull, I know – I'm currently thinking up an exotic middle name, got any ideas?) It's great to meet you and I can tell we're going to get along just great!

Me and my friends, Flower, Bubble, Missy and Princess (aka the Best Mates), love thinking up ways we can improve the everyday lives of girlkind throughout this planet we call "Earth". (Why we gave our own bit of the universe such a boring name and wasted brilliant names like Venus on other bits is beyond me.) But anyway, to get back to what I was saying, if you're looking for top-quality advice sprinkled with the odd rubbish joke, then look no further than right here! It is our mission to serve you, oh Earth maiden!

Before I introduce you to the rest of the Best Mates, here's a bit more about me:

**Full name:** Molly ____ (insert exciting middle-name suggestion here) White
**Distinguishing features:** Dazzling beauty and huge brain!

(OK, I've got brown sticky-out hair, I'm a bit short and my nerdy teachers reckon I've got "potential"!)

**Family history:** One male parent (Dad), one female parent (Mum) and one incredibly annoying, very stupid twin brother (Billy = spotty male). We reside in a boring town I call Dullsville, located in the county of Spamshire.

**Life would be utterly dull without:** Long words, chocolate, poetry, most music and hanging out in my bedroom with the Mates.

**Pet peeves:** Stupid people, pollution, Brussels sprouts (one question: why?) and uninvited snoopers entering my bedroom (especially ones called Billy).

**Current bedroom decor:** Relaxed bohemian vibe (OK, it's really messy), walls painted deep, dark purple and midnight blue, with gold stars on the ceiling, bulging bookcases and lots of big velvet cushions and throws.

Over to you now, Best Mates – tell our new Mate all about yourselves!

_Flower_

**AKA:** Flower Spirit Delaney (Molly: "Now, _that's_ what I call a groovy middle name!")

**Life would be utterly dull without:** "Nature! I adore all animals and wildlife. And I'm really into aromatherapy, feng shui and stuff like that."

**Pet peeves:** "Cruelty to animals, and bullying."

**Fave bedroom feature:** "My canopy bed!"

* * * * * * * * * * * * * *

_Bubble_

**AKA:** Cybil Bubridge (Molly: "And I moan about _my_ name!")

**Life would be utterly dull without:** "Having a laugh with the Mates, shouting, running (I'm the top sprinter in my school – boast!), scoffing pizzas and really, really loud music."

**Pet peeves:** "Wusses and having to share a bedroom with my soppy little sister."

**Fave bedroom feature:** "The collage of photos me and the Mates have made over the years!"

## Missy

**AKA:** Nora Baxter (Molly: "We only ever call her Missy though!")

**Life would be utterly dull without:** "My mobile, R&B music, cool clothes, and gossip!"

**Pet peeves:** "A low battery, oh, and too much homework, 'cos it gets in the way of my busy social schedule!"

**Fave bedroom feature:** "My funky orange and black colour scheme!"

* * * * * * * * * * * * * * * * * * * * *

## Princess

**AKA:** Pandora Elizabeth Alexandra Moxbury (Molly: "How many posh names can one girl have, eh?!")

**Life would be utterly dull without:** "Shopping, art, painting and glossy magazines."

**Pet peeves:** "Untidiness, having no money and mean people."

**Fave bedroom feature:** "'The Salon' – well that's what we Mates call it – it's just my dressing table really, but it's crammed with beauty products and it's where we spend hours doing makeovers!"

8

So your room needs a blitz, huh? Luckily you've come to the right place. This book is bursting with the best blitzing tips and latest lush looks for cool bedrooms. Read on and we'll show you how to:

★ Persuade your parents to do things *your* way!
★ Turn a dull room into a dazzling dream-palace!
★ Free your inner artist and become a sensational style queen, greatly admired by all you meet!

All those in favour of joining the Best Mates on their intrepid voyage into bedroom-blitzing, turn the page now!

Congratulations, Mate, you're in! Now, as you're officially one of us, it's my pleasure to offer you our sacred pledge:

The Best Mates' pledge

1. To be on hand with our expert advice 24/7, sleeping by your side if necessary.

★

2. To never get the hump with you — even if you completely ignore our advice.

★

3. To never hardly ever snigger at your many, many mistakes, mad fads and truly bonkers brainwaves.

★

4. Basically, you have our undying love, loyalty blah de blah de blah and can borrow any of our things, any time ... for eternity!

Hmm. With a lick of gold paint, that pledge would look lovely hung above your bed. Ooh, hark at me, I've started already! That must mean it's time for our first chapter...

# Let the Blitzing Begin!

**"** First up, let's take a moment to really love our bedrooms! **"**

**"** Uh-oh! Flower's having one of her hippy-dippy moments! **"**

**"** No, seriously! My mum, who I admit is a bit of a hippy, told me before I did up my room that I had to really think about what I used my 'space' for and to really appreciate it. That way I would know how to 'style' it. **"**

That sounds reasonable. I love my room 'cos it's where my beloved bed is, and I do like my ZZZZs! Mates, why do you love your bedrooms?

11

**"I can do my own thing without being spied on!"**

**"Because it's where I go to think about things."**

**"It's where I keep all my gear."**

its where me & tha m8s chill

> **❝**OK, so bedrooms are great! Now grab the glitter paint, Mate, and let's decorate!**❞**

Hmm, nice rapping, Bubble, but before our Mate starts slapping paint around like a loon, she's got to have worked out her answers to three very important little questions, which we shall call:

## The BM's pre-blitz triple challenge!

OK, so I've given this bit a fancy-pants title to disguise the fact that this is where you have to think sensibly about the three key things before you begin your bedroom makeover.

**WATCH IT, Mate!** We must warn you that failure to think about these three practical considerations will mean you'll be destined to live forever in a pit of disorganized chaos, with zero style and really naff furniture chosen by your mum when you were, like, five!

## Sensible thought 1: How can I get my parents' permission?

**"**Oh, I can help with this bit! I've become something of an expert in the field of problem-parent persuading, having had many years practising on two particularly stubborn specimens – my mum and dad!**"**

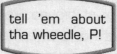

tell 'em about tha wheedle, P!

**"**Ah, yes, The Wheedle is a special sneaky tactic that we BMs use to persuade or trick our parents into letting us have what we want. Let me demonstrate… You will note that I've included two kinds of wheedle. The average parent can usually be persuaded using the mini wheedle, but if they're being majorly stubborn you might have to use more extreme action – the major wheedle. Look out for more Persuaders as we go!**"**

# Princess's Parent Persuader No 1

YOU WANT: to makeover your bedroom.

THE PARENTS WANT: you to leave things as they are.

TYPICAL PARENT QUOTE: "But your room's very pretty as it is and anyway I thought you liked fluffy bunny rabbits."

MINI WHEEDLE: Show them not only that you've moved on since your room was last done (circa a gubillion years ago) but also that you are sensible and responsible by bagging up all the things in your room that you've grown out of - old dolls, clothes, etc - and tell them you'd like to give them to the local charity shop. Finally, win them over by showing them your super-organized plans for your bedroom revamp.

MAJOR WHEEDLE: Make a promise that if you are allowed to makeover your room you will keep it tidy for ever - mums are unable to refuse this offer. However, if you still face resistance, you could plead that a new-look bedroom would very probably inspire greater homework productivity.

Nice wheedling, Princess! Once you've sorted out The Parents and got their permission for an all-out bedroom blitz, the next thing to do is to plan your budget and schedule.

**"Yawnsville!"**

**"Don't listen, Mate! Bubble tried to skip this bit when she was revamping her room, and she ended up having to paint her walls *after* her new shelves had been put up – she got paint everywhere! And then she blew her budget on takeaway pizza for us Mates, which meant she never got her room finished!"**

**"I'm gonna get around to it soon, no probs!"**

Yeah, right! The choice is yours, Mate. Do you want to be a Bumblesome Bubble or a Sorted Sister?

Right, all of you wannabe Sorted Sisters, grab your purse and prepare to count those precious pennies!

## Sensible thought 2: How much money have I got?

Once you've counted up your pennies (yes, even the sticky fluffy ones from the back of the sofa) and worked out how much money you've got, it's time to start thinking about what you can realistically afford to do with it. If your penny pile is a bit piddly, go for a few trendy tweaks rather than a ballistic blitz – and don't worry, whatever your budget, we Mates have thought of loads of top tips for sassing up your space!

Before you begin your blitz, you should try to get an idea of how much things cost – check out prices in magazines and catalogues as well as shops. If something you want turns out to be mega expensive, suss out a cheaper idea.

wot if r mate has no pennies, not even sticky fluffy 1s?!

Try asking your parents to make a cash "donation" to your worthy cause...

# Princess's Parent Persuader No 2

YOU WANT: cash for your blinding new bedroom blitz

THE PARENTS WANT: to spend no more than two pee (or thereabouts)

TYPICAL PARENT QUOTE: "You seem to think we're made of money!" or "It doesn't grow on trees, y'know!"

MINI WHEEDLE: Explain that you plan to do your blitz really cheaply, and have hunted out the most bargainous prices in town. Then present your modest budget calculations – how could they fail to help out such a sensible young lady?!

MAJOR WHEEDLE: Drive them potty with your constant pocket money-making schemes (eg, polishing dad's shoes while he's still wearing them, walking the dog until the poor beast is pooped, making undrinkably strong cups of tea, etc). With any luck, they'll finance your revamp just to keep you out of their way!

**Best Mates TOP TIP**

Even if a cash crisis means that your budget is precisely nought pence, don't worry. It's amazing how much you can transform your bedroom by something as simple as rearranging the furniture or revamping your old junk (see Bubble's tips on page 72).

**"**Well, that's the dosh and The Parents sorted, we're r-r-ready to r-r-revamp!!!**"**

H-h-hold your giddy galloping horses, Bumblesome! We've not covered the thing you always run out of yet ... time!

## Sensible thought 3: How much time have I got?

It's important to set a realistic amount of time aside to complete your makeover. So while you won't want to rush things, you also don't want things to drag on or be in danger of being abandoned 'cos you've got bored with it! A weekend seems a reasonable amount of time for a good blitz. Also make sure you schedule it for a time when you won't be bothered by homework worries – eg, during school holidays – and when a parent can be on hand, in case you need their help.

Once you've sussed out when you're going to do your revamp, next up is the even more muddlesome business of working out what order you should do things in and how long it's going to take to finish each job.

66 The only bit of sensible advice I've ever got from my dodgy 'DIY expert' father is that you should estimate how long each task will take – then double it! 99

Hey, Flower, to show our Mate an example of how she could timetable her blitz – could you dig out the plans we Mates made when we helped with your two-day bedroom blitz?!"

66 Oh you mean The Sorted Sister Schedule! Good idea. I'd have been lost without my SSS! First of all, though, our Mate should know the seven steps I took to turn my dull, cutesy bedroom into a sophisticated den for a happening chick (that's me!) and her cool pals! Here's my original 'To Do' list: 99

1. Paint mural on one wall to add "wow" factor

2. Create chill-out zone using huge floor cushions

3. Make study area by replacing old chest of drawers with new desk

4. Buy cheap boxes for funky storage

5. Paint window frame and inside of door

6. Make floaty canopy over the bed for extra sophistication

7. Have teddy cull to go with sophisticated new look

8. Replace old babyish wardrobe with groovy mini clothes rail

# Flower's Sorted Sister Schedule

| Time | Task |
| --- | --- |
| *Day 1:* 10 am | General preparation:<br>Clear away all clutter<br>Protect all surfaces with old sheets |
| 11 am | Painting:<br>Draw mural outline<br>Prepare window and door frame for painting – then paint on first coat<br>Start painting mural |
| 4 pm | Make floor cushions |
| *Day 2:* 10 am | More painting:<br>Do second coat (if necessary) on window and door<br>Finish painting mural |

**66**I chose a weekend to complete my bedroom blitz, with an extra day the weekend before to buy all the stuff I needed. Here's how I timetabled the blitz – as we went along, I ticked off all the jobs one by one.**99**

| | |
|---|---|
| 2 pm | Make canopy above bed |
| 3 pm | Rearrange and tidy:<br>Remove old sheets<br>Take clothes from old wardrobe and arrange on new rail and in stacking boxes – have old wardrobe removed<br>Arrange floor cushions under bed<br>Create study area on new desk<br>Store some teddies away (sob!) |
| 5 pm | Ta-daa! Stand amazed at sight of blitzed bedroom! |

**"**Man, you were so organized!
I remember you even had a
clipboard – serious or what?!?
I never had anything like that
when I did my room!**"**

Erm, maybe that's why yours went a bit wrong,
Bubble?!? Doing a budget and a schedule is essential
for keeping a bedroom blitz on the right track. Once
they're sorted, then the fun, creative bits can begin!

**"**Yippeee! I lurrve the
creative bits!**"**

# Themes, Schemes and BluePrints

We hope you've got those creative brain juices flowing, Mate, 'cos in this chapter we are going to help you:

★ Identify your own very special style
★ Learn everything there is to know about colour
★ Plan a design for your fabulous new boudoir (posh French for dreamy girly bedroom!).

Let's start with the "style" thing...
Whether you're planning a total new look for your bedroom or just a few tweaks here and there, you're going to want it done in a style that suits you, that reflects your tastes and says something about gorgeous little old YOU!

**❝And just how do you know what your 'style' is?!❞**

25

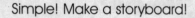

Simple! Make a storyboard!

> **❝**I saw one of those swanky designers on the TV do one of these, but he called his a 'mood-maker'!**❞**

Call it what you will, but a storyboard is basically a big bit of card filled with loads of pictures which you can use as inspiration for your revamp. Here's how to make one:

## How to make your very own style-sussing storyboard

First get together the following:

★ A big bit of card ★ As many magazines, brochures and catalogues as you can get hold of. (Don't pinch your mum's without asking though – it's not worth the hassle!) ★ Glue ★ Scissors

Next: flick through the magazines, cutting out any pictures you fancy. They can be pictures of rooms, people, places, objects or even just colours. The important thing is that they should all reflect your tastes.

26

For example, you could choose pictures of cool people whose style you admire, groovy bits of furniture you like the look of or even a T-shirt you like the colour of.

Then: stick all your cutouts on to your card – placing them either higgedly-piggedly to make one big collage or into sections, with one area for your favourite colours, one for fabulous furniture, etc.

Finally: use your finished storyboard to inspire your fabulous new bedroom. For example, if your storyboard is full of pinks and pics of sparkly objects, perhaps a pink palace of girly loveliness is the boudoir for you! Or if you've chosen lots of shots of glamorous  movie stars and stylish homes for your storyboard, then a sophisticated den with bold colours and lots of luxury, velvety fabrics is maybe your kinda thing.

But before you go loopy with the glitter or the velvet, Missy's thought of four very handy rules to make sure your chosen theme really is the right one for you.

## 4 roolz 4 picking a theme
*by "on tha mobile" missy*

rool 1 go 4 somthin that suits yr personality; if u r a couch potato, a sports theme won't suit u!

rool 2 also get inspired by yr own stuff – eg, if u collect alien-themed gear, consider a futuristic look

rool 3 don't be a slave 2 1 theme – if yr storyboard has more than 1 theme, think about how u can make them work 2gether!

rool 4 think about how easy yr chosen look will b 2 live with (day-glo orange walls can turn a mellow m8 in2 a grumpy grouch on sunny early mornings!) & if it will look dated 2 soon

Once you've decided on a theme that's right for you, the next step is to decide on a colour scheme. Although your storyboard will contain colours that inspire you, Flower's here to make doubly sure you're making the right choices with her handy guide to the world of colour.

# What hue are you?

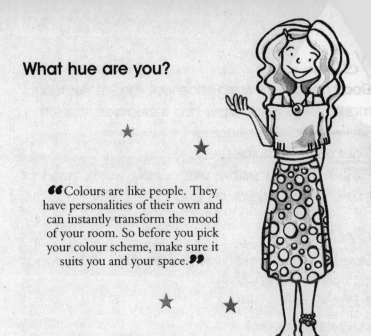

**"**Colours are like people. They have personalities of their own and can instantly transform the mood of your room. So before you pick your colour scheme, make sure it suits you and your space.**"**

## WARM COLOURS

Warm, deep colours like red, reddy-purple, orange and yellow give rooms an intimate, snug feel.

## Red

*Good points:* brings passion, drama and life and makes bigger rooms inviting and intimate

*Bad vibe:* makes small rooms seem smaller and stuffy

*Goes well with:* green and gold

*People who like red are:* passionate, curious and very bold

*points:* sunny and cheerful, brightens dull rooms, making them seem larger, and is creatively stimulating
*Bad vibe:* not very peaceful
*Goes well with:* purples
*People who like yellow are:* bubbly, warm, good at talking and making others laugh, and sporty

## Orange

*Good points:* bold, lively and fun, encourages conversation and eating!
*Bad vibe:* not very restful
*Goes well with:* blue
*People who like orange are:* charming, attention-seeking but very kind-hearted

## Pink

*Good points:* uplifting, soothing and welcoming
*Bad vibes:* can look a bit cutesy
*Goes well with:* pale green or lilac
*People who like pink are:* very affectionate, gentle and everyone's friend

# Princess's Parent Persuader No 3

YOU WANT: wild and wacky colours

THE PARENTS WANT: boring and dull or no changes at all

TYPICAL PARENT QUOTE: "Pink is so unpractical, oatmeal will look lovely, you'll see."

MINI WHEEDLE: Agree to keep the walls plain but suggest your choice of paint for the woodwork

MAJOR WHEEDLE: Wage a campaign by cornering each parent individually and relentlessly asking stuff like, "If you were me, what colour scheme would you have, pink or purple?" Sooner or later one of them will slip and say "Pink", then you've got them! Sort of...

# COOL COLOURS

Lighter, cooler shades like green, blue, bluey-purple and white give rooms a spacious, elegant feel; and so are especially good if you want your piddly box room to look bigger.

# Blue

*Good points:* symbolizes loyalty and brings harmony, peace and comfort

*Bad vibe:* can seem cold

*Goes well with:* orange

*People who like blue are:* honest, confident and brilliant listeners

# Green

*Good points:* the colour of nature – it is refreshing and promotes spiritual awareness (or so my hippy mum says!)

*Bad vibes:* darker shades can be dull

*Goes well with:* red

*People who like green are:* mothering types who like to make sure everyone, including themselves, feels fine physically and emotionally

# Purple

*Good points:* strong, powerful and thought-provoking

*Bad vibes:* a bit intense

*Goes well with:* yellow

*People who like purple are:* very independent, sensitive and a bit secretive

## Beginning to plan your new bedroom

So, you've got your theme sorted and your colours selected and it's almost time to put pencil to paper. But hold it right there – before you begin, there are still a few important things to bear in mind.

Even if you've only got a small room, you can make the most of the space by "zoning"...

sounds more like something you do to a car park than a bedroom!

Ahem. I'll have you know that creating "zones" in your bedroom will not only make it look really cool, it will help you get super-organized! All you do is start by thinking about all the things you do in your room: sleeping, relaxing, entertaining, dressing, beautifying, etc.

Each activity should be given a set place – or "zone" in your room where you can arrange all the supplies and furniture you need to do it. For example, Princess has created "The Salon" in her room where we do our beauty makeovers. It's centred on her dressing table and chair, and she keeps all her hair, make-up and accessories there. Nearly everything in The Salon is pink!

Don't worry if your room is small – just give one zone two functions! For example, my girly gossiping zone (four floor cushions plonked on the floor by the door) is also my dressing-up zone. (It's by my clothes rail, the door has a full-length mirror on the back and there's plenty of room for posing in front of the mirror when the cushions are stuffed back under the bed.)

Repositioning your furniture is a great way of creating zones. For example, moving your bed into the middle of the room (if it's big enough) will give you zones on either side of the bed.

**"** And then the bed can be your focal point. According to the swanky home improvement mags my mum reads, all the best-designed rooms have focal points or FPs. This is when you emphasize a key feature in your room, so when someone walks in they immediately look at the FP and go, "Wowweeee!" You can make fab FPs by painting a huge mural, putting fairy lights around your window or piling your bed high with fluffy cushions – just use your imagination! **"**

OK, so how are you visualizing your new room? Is it a swanky, palace-like pad filled with expensive gear and a luxury bed the size of a football pitch? Yeah? Uh-oh, Mate, it sounds like you need to get real about what you can actually achieve with your modest little bedroom. We're talking facing up to some basic practical considerations – start by taking part in this small quizlet:

## The "have you gone a bit bedroom-blitz bonkers?" test

Honest answers only please…

**1** Is your bedroom big enough for your fabulous revamp?

**2** Have you included essential stuff like your bed, desk and wardrobe in your plans?

**3** Is there enough money in Mr Piggy to cover your costs?

**4** Are you still going to be able to comfortably sleep, get dressed, do your homework, have friends around and just chill in your new room?

If you answered a happy "yes" to all of the above you may proceed to the next bit! Any of you who muttered a sulky "no" will have to sit in a darkened room until your crazy wee brain calms down and comes up with something less fantastical.

## The next bit

OK, Mate, let's get ready to put all your braintastic thoughts into action – yes, it's blueprint time! But don't worry, Mate, you don't have to be an artistic genius. As long as you can operate a pencil and ruler you'll be fine! The idea of making a blueprint is to help you get organized, making sure you've thought of everything you'll need for your new room, and to give you a rough idea of what the end result is going to look like – it's not a drawing competition!

> **❝**I love this bit – it's where you get to be really arty making groovy illustrations of how your new room's going to look – just like one of those proper designers from the telly!**❞**

## How to make your blueprint
### You will need:

★ A few sheets of A4 paper – graph paper if you've got it
★ Measuring tape ★ Ruler ★ Pencil and rubber (even the pros make constant revisions!) ★ Coloured pens or card
★ Frilly shirt (ha! not really – unless you actually *want* to look like a super poseur designer-type, that is!)

### What you do:

**1** Measure your bedroom – don't forget to do all the walls, windows and doorway.

**2** Also measure larger items like your bed, desk and chest of drawers.

**3** Start plotting the layout and contents of your new room on to the paper. Make sure you draw your bedroom to scale. (To draw something to scale, try using 5 cm in your drawing to represent 1 metre in real life. You can adjust this figure to make your drawing bigger or smaller.)

**4** Using coloured pens, or, even better, those colour charts you get free at paint shops, indicate what colours you plan to use where. You don't need to go mad colouring in, just draw or cut out a small coloured square and put it to the side of your blueprint, then use arrows or a numbering system to indicate where the colour will go – this is the way the pros do it!

To give you an idea of what your blueprint could look like, take a peek at the one we did when we were planning how to do up Flower's room.

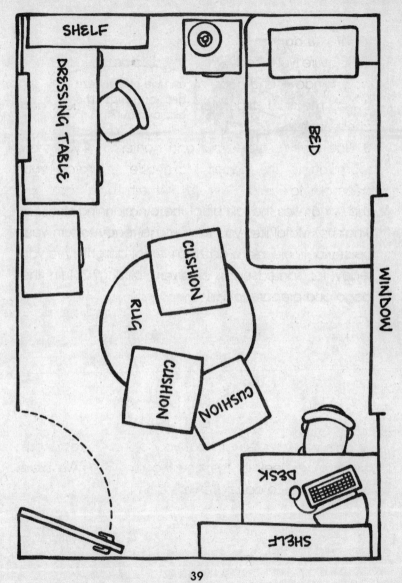

SHELF

DRESSING TABLE

BED

RUG

CUSHION

CUSHION

CUSHION

WINDOW

DESK

SHELF

39

can we pleeeeeeze get on with the blitzing now?!

Yup – that was the last bit of the pre-planning stuff! So, whatsup, Mate? Do you think you're ready to turn your belchy bolthole into a dazzling den of delight?! Are you ready for some serious bedroom-blitzing?!? Turn the page and prepare to DIY!

# Ultimate Bedroom Makeovers

I know there will be some of you out there who are grumbling, "Create a dream boudoir out of my piffling, shoe box-sized pit?! Pah! Impossible!"

Well, listen up, grumblers, 'cos we BMs have spent hours, days and sometimes even whole maths lessons thinking about this, and have come up with some easy-to-follow guides to help you create your dream boudoir! Exciting, huh?

Before you know it, your bedroom will be the envy of your friends, relatives, neighbours, and the worlds of fashion, music and TV. Indeed, don't be surprised if Hollywood calls asking to film the story of your bedroom's creation! Ha!

## Three dream boudoirs for dreamy babes (er, that's you, Mate!)

### Molly's moochy–mocha!

Have you noticed just how many coffee shops there are now?!? (Answer: Heaps!) I love the ones with all the saggy sofas, dim, atmospheric lighting, and deep dark red walls. They just look such a neat place to hang out – either just by yourself reading or chillin' with friends. Anyway, that's what inspired this look.

**Theme:** Coffee-shop chic
**Best for:** Large rooms
**Would appeal to:** Deep-thinking, sophisticated Mates who love to read or have intelligent conversations with their chums.
**Colour scheme:** Rich burgundy red on walls, and chocolatey brown on woodwork.
**Special effects:** Use gold metallic felt-tip pens to draw loads of hearts and stars – or whatever you want – all around the walls. (It looks arty and breaks up the heaviness of the dark colours.)
**Luxury feature/focal point:** The Zen Zone – special zone designed for entertaining your friends or for moments of

quiet thought! To do the ZZ, get a small, low coffee table (an upturned fruit crate or sturdy box with a fancy covering will do!) and surround it with floor cushions. (See page 79 for how to make cushions.)

**Added extras:** Interesting reading material laid out on coffee table (like this book!), and rich aromas using coffee-scented candles or incense. (Note the "Watch it, Mate" on p49.)

★ **Blitzer bitz!** ★
*Sensationally clever things to do with walls*

★ Paint each wall a different colour – it'll make your room look bigger and more interesting.

★ Draw out features like chimney breasts and recesses by painting them in a contrasting colour to the rest of your room.

★ You can get some brilliant wrapping paper designs; find one you like and cover one wall or area with it, using Blu-tack to put it up – ta-daa, instant groovy wallpaper!

★ Let your room express your personality by displaying bits of artwork you've made yourself – be proud, you artistic genius you!

★ Turn one wall into a "photo gallery" – visitors will never tire of teasing you about your "cute" baby photos!

# Princess and her chamber of magick!

**❝**I love all this witchy themed stuff which is soooo trendy at the mo! Here, I've been inspired by all things magical and spooky, with a helping hand from some leftover Halloween party gear.**❞**

**Theme:** Olde worlde witchy chic

**Best for:** Medium-sized or attic rooms

**Would appeal to:** Sensitive, independent-minded Mates with a strong sense of drama!

**Colour scheme:** Paint your walls purple (v mystical and spiritual apparently), unless your room is small, then think about painting one or two of the other walls in a lighter colour – like goldy yellow – to stop the room feeling too stuffy. Then, to give it that authentic gothic castle touch, paint any woodwork, doors, etc, in dark grey or black gloss.

**Special effects:** Along the top of your walls, paint a frieze of the cycle of the moon, using luminous white or glow-in-the-dark paint. Go gradually from new moon to full moon – using about eight "moons" for each cycle. Repeat until you come back to where you started from.

You can paint your moons any size, but about 30 cm in diameter is a nice, eye-catching size.

**Luxury feature/focal point:** Turn your boring bed into a magical, "flying" snooze-palace! Here's how:

*Start by making a very elaborate and gothic, but super-easy-to-make headboard.*

**1** Move your bed into a central-ish position in your bedroom, but so the head of the bed is pushed up against a wall (preferably one that's painted purple).

**2** Using easy-to-rub-off chalk and a ruler, draw a line on the wall where the top of the mattress lies.

**3** Move the bed out of the way, and cover surfaces – messy painting bit about to happen.

**4** Still using the chalk, design an elaborate headboard, using your original chalk line as the "base" of your headboard. Try a fancy scrolly type like this one.

**5** Now use paint to fill in your headboard outline – black paint will give it an olde-worlde wrought iron look, or use a light colour, like gold, if you want it to stand out more.

*And now for the "flying" part:*

**1** Either buy or make a bed skirt from see-through material (netting is fine) and put it around your bed, so that it tumbles down from the bottom of your mattress to the floor. (The easiest way to make a bed skirt is get a large piece of material and lay it squarely over your bed base, then put your mattress back on top. For an average-sized single bed, your material should be approximately 180 cm wide and 250 cm long – which allows for a drop of about 40 cm for the "skirt" part.)

**2** Place fairy lights under the netting around your bed – the netting makes the lights fuzzy and spooky – like your bed is hovering above the ground!

**Added extras:** Use things like fake spiders, owls, mice and cobwebs leftover from Halloween, old coloured bottles, candles and candle-holders to give an even witchier atmosphere to your room.

## Princess's parent persuader No 4

**YOU WANT:** fancy effects – a canopy bed, mural of stars, bejewelled mirror, etc

**THE PARENTS WANT:** to keep things straight and simple

**TYPICAL PARENT QUOTE:** "You're not putting all that junk in your room!"

**MINI WHEEDLE:** Show them how great these things can look with pictures cut from magazines or printed from the Internet.

**MAJOR WHEEDLE:** Flatter them into helping you with your fancy effects (eg, "But you're so very good at sewing, etc). They'll end up being proud of the "junk" they've helped make!

# Bubble's amazing Amazon

**❝**'Cos I have to share my room with my little sis, we're always arguing about what our room should look like – she likes cute fluffy animals whereas I like to think about wild, exotic places and saving the planet! Anyway, we decided to compromise by going for a jungle theme which included all our fave things.**❞**

**Theme:** Wild jungle mayhem

**Best for:** Small or shared rooms

**Would appeal to:** Frustrated Mates desperate for an end to the ongoing war with really annoying sibling and/or a very outgoing, spontaneous kind of Mate with "adventurous" tastes.

**Colour scheme:** Oranges, greens and animal-print patterns.

**Special effects:** Cover *everything* with animal-print fun fur (go for "tiger" rather than "cow" though!). For instance, make your own cushion covers (see page 79), or glue fun fur on to things like your bin or the back of your door.

**Luxury feature/focal point:** Add a fringe of exotic jungle vines dangling down one wall and a cute tree-top canopy! Here's how to do it:

**1** Paint one wall intense jungle green.

**2** Ask Dad or Mum to help you put up a row of shelves near the top of the wall.

**3** To make your vines, cut about 20 5 cm x 150 cm lengths of green-coloured felt (although you could use other material or some strong string instead).

**4** Secure your vines with drawing pins along the underside of your shelf.

**5** Cover your shelves with more green felt (or other material) so that it flops over the lip of your shelves and the tops of your vines, and tack it down with drawing pins.

Ta-daaa! A comfy tree-top canopy for all your (or your annoying sis's) cuddly toys to romp around on!

(Tip: I also got a few of my sis's cuddly monkeys, spiders, snakes, etc and tied them at various heights on to the vines – even I'll admit they look cute!)

**Added extra:** Show you care about conservation by pinning up a world map with the world's diminishing jungles and endangered species highlighted. (Check out the World Wildlife Fund Internet site for further information.)

That's it for the dreamiest of the dreamy boudoirs, BMs. Now how about doing three new looks on no (or very little) money? Take it away, girls!

## Three cheap 'n' easy radical revamps

# Missy's chillin' oriental chamber

i like this look cos it looks v modern, neat, clean & bright. 2 get it right, just think about keeping things simple & using loadsa natural stuff, like plain fabrics, wood and stone

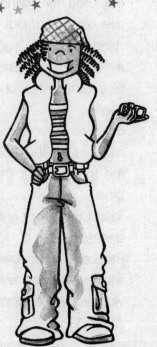

**preparation:** clear out all yr clutter (see flower's feng shui tips on page 63)

**bed:** 4 that japanese-style low bed look, see if yr parents will let u take off the legs on yr bed (if it's got em!) or 4 an even lower bed, see if they'll remove the base unit & let u just have tha mattress on tha floor! (watch out 4 spiders tho!)

**colour scheme:** keep the colour theme as simple as u can: no patterned stuff – just blocks of neutral colours, like cream, beige, white and black

**windows:** 2 give yr room a bright hazy glow, make some beautifully simple japanese-style curtains: get 2 pieces of cheap white muslin (each 1 should be half the width of yr window but twice as long). then put one end of each "curtain" over a net curtain rod or curtain pole, and gently pull it down so that it is evenly doubled over. do the same with the other curtain. alter the mood of yr room with different-coloured muslin

**lights:** get 1 of those huge, round paper lampshades 4 yr overhead light

**walls:** chinese & japanese writing looks really

cool & arty – either get hold of some stencils & use them around yr walls (if yr allowed) or copy the 1s printed here using black paint. copy them on 2 white sheets of paper, pop them in clip-frames and hang them around yr room

**accessories:** collect lots of natural objects like twigs, stones & shells & display them simply around yr room – long twigs look groovy in a big vase. also, has mum got a couple of house plants u can borrow? (palms & cacti r easy 2 look after & r v stylish!)

# Flower's hippy hangout

**66**Getting the hippy look is really simple. I came up with this revamp idea simply by copying the best bits from our house! The look basically has a retro 1960s feel to it, and involves lots of things to do with caring about the environment, peace, love and flower power. You'll like this best if you're naturally laid-back, a bit unconventional and enjoy cosy, welcoming spaces!**99**

**Preparation:** Think peaceful thoughts to get in the right groove, man!

**Bed:** Cover your bed with a homely patchwork quilt, woolly bedspread or flowery duvet. If you haven't got anything suitable, try tie-dyeing a sheet (see page 91) to go over your bed.

**Colour scheme:** Go for soulful pale purples and calming greens. If you want to add the odd splash of pattern go for something psychedelic (a wild mix of lots of bright colours).

**Windows:** String some brightly coloured plastic beads or crystals on to various lengths of nylon thread (with knots at the end) and hang your bejewelled beauties from the top of your window, using a pin or Blu-tack, so they dangle in front of the window pane. During the day your beauties will catch the sun and send shimmers of coloured light around your room.

**Walls:** Make some groovy wall hangings by getting a huge piece of plain cloth (muslin is cheap and looks nice and floaty) and painting designs on it with fabric paint. Try painting on huge flower heads, the peace sign or a slogan about something you feel strongly about (eg: Stop cruelty to animals now!) to go with your hippy theme; or, again, you could simply tie-dye your hangings.

**Furniture:** Get the laid-back hippy vibe by getting in a few big, comfy floor cushions so you and your mates can sit around and just chill and chat (see page 79 for directions on how to make floor cushions).

**Accessories:** A wind chime located near your door will give a mystical tinkle when your door is opened or closed. If your budget won't stretch to a chime, scented candles and pongy incense will add to the hippy vibe.

# Princess's angelic slumber palace

**❝**This is my sophisticated version of a theme that uses lots of images of angels, stars and clouds. It should make you feel as though you've walked into a little bit of heaven – literally!**❞**

**Preparation:** Give your room a thorough clean – dust, sticky fizzy drink stains and smelly socks are not what you expect to find when you open heaven's gate!

**Bed:** To make your bed seem like it's floating among the clouds, make it into a fluffy heap with as many cushions and pillows (preferably with white covers) as you can find in the house. Then make a white muslin bed

...e it using angels and stars – I like gold ... use whatever you can get. (See page 73 ... s advice on using stencils, page 87 for how to ... a bed canopy and page 79 for cushion-making.)

**Colour scheme:** Sky blue and fluffy cloud white, of course! Plus lots of gold-coloured accessories.

**Lights:** A huge white paper lantern used overhead will give a nice, clear white light – it'll be just like being in heaven!

**Walls:** A brilliant idea is to write something like "dream" or "angel" in as many different languages as you can find (try searching on the Internet – www.free-translator.com is a good site!) all over your walls.

Do it using a small paintbrush and in your fanciest handwriting. It looks really arty if you use the same colour as the paint on your walls, but just a shade or two lighter or darker.

**Ceiling:** Stick up loads of self-adhesive glow-in-the-dark stars or paint stars and moons using any spare paint you've got.

**Accessories:** Get as many angel-themed things as you can find. Plaster-cast cherubs spray-painted gold look brilliant! If you have, like, *no* money, have a rummage in the Christmas decorations and see what suitable stuff you can find.

The great thing about these quick-fix ideas is that they are so easy, cheap and versatile you could change the look of your room almost as often as Princess does if you wanted to!

**❝**I'll have you know that I've actually had the angelic look for three whole months! I can't wait to create my next theme though!**❞**

How about you, Mate? Got your creative vision yet? Sorted your schedule? Sketched your blueprint? Don't worry if you haven't, we Best Mates have still got bags more ideas and magical makeover tips for you – and we're not going anywhere until you get it together!

And if you never get it together? Well I suppose you could always let YOUR MOTHER DO UP YOUR BEDROOM!!!

Ha! Not really, I just said that so you'd realize what's at risk here! COME ON!

# Making the Most of What You've Got

So, Mate, do you want an eye-bogglingly brilliant bedroom but feel thwarted by an empty purse, parent power or lack of time. Or do you simply feel uninspired by your piddly box room? Have no fear, Mate, 'cos we're here to look at some really simple ways of turning your drab dorm into a fab pad!

**❝**My big problem is keeping my room tidy. My little sis is *the* messiest minx and let's just say housework doesn't come naturally to me!**❞**

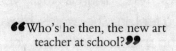

**❝**That's because you've not been following the teachings of feng shui (pronounced: fung shway).**❞**

**❝**Who's he then, the new art teacher at school?**❞**

**66** No, silly! It's an ancient Chinese philosophy that teaches you how to live in harmony with your environment. **99**

**66** Uh-oh, I feel a lesson in feng shui coming on! **99**

## A quick lesson in feng shui

★ Feng shui is spookily old – dating back to China about 5,000 years ago.

★ It means wind (no, not the burping kind, Bubble!) and water, 'cos that's what people had to be aware of when building their homes (eg, not to build somewhere too windy or prone to flooding).

★ The basic principle of feng shui is that your surroundings affect how you feel. In other words, messy, smelly, poorly designed living spaces don't make you a happy bunny!

★ An example of feng shui at work in your bedroom would be to use a vibrant colour like orange around your desk to help you to find the brain-power to do your homework, and a soft relaxing colour like green around your bed area to help soothe you to sleep.

★ In feng shui, there are lots of odd rules based on old superstitions about how rooms and houses should be laid out. But behind the superstitions you can actually find a lot of great, modern design tips. Like these:

**Rule 1:** Don't position your bed so that your feet point directly towards the door.

**Superstition:** This is known as the "death position" in China, 'cos dead people are always carried out feet first – it's therefore reckoned to be bad luck.

**Design tip:** Opening the door and seeing a bed in a straight line in front of you is pretty boring (and a bit draughty!). Try to create more interesting angles for your bed when you're planning the layout of your room.

**Rule 2:** Never place your desk so that your back is to the door.

**Superstition:** Sitting with your back to the door makes you open to attacks from "back-stabbers".

**Design tip:** It will make your work area seem less cramped if you sit with a wall behind you and face out into your room. Also, being able to see your door from your desk will mean The Parents can't catch you in the act of *not* doing your homework!

66 Now then, Bubble, let me tell you and our Mate how feng shui can help you sort out a messy room.

66 One of the ideas of feng shui is that everything should have a home, and that if your space is a mess, you won't be able to find anything, you'll get frustrated and your ch'i (Chinese for your inner energy) will be pooped! 99

## Six steps to decluttering your bedroom by Flower (and her pal feng shui!)

**1** Get three bin liners: one for junk to throw away; one for stuff to give to charity; and one for stuff that needs to find a home.

**2** Sort through all your stuff, asking yourself three questions:

**a)** Do I love it? ★

**b)** Do I really need it? ★

**c)** Is it useful?

Anything which gets two "not really"s should be binned – except if you think it might be useful to someone else, then give it to charity.

**3** If you haven't used something for over two years – face it, you don't need it! Get rid of it now!

**4** Keep the mess under control by having a mini tidy every day (putting away clothes, homework, etc). Promise yourself to do five minutes' worth every night before bedtime.

**5** Keep work spaces and dressing tables clear of stuff that you don't use on a weekly basis.

**6** Give each possession a definite home; even if it's under your bed, as long as it's organized and dust-free, that's fine!

Hey Mate! Now you've turned your pig-sty into a, erm, sty-lish pad, want to know the secret of keeping it that way for ever with very little effort?!? Yeah? Well according to Missy it's all about storage...

## store and stash with missy!

### shelve it

☺ get dad 2 build loads of shelves!

☺ put stuff u use a lot lower down on the shelves so u can reach it easily & bung stuff u don't use so much up top

### box it

☺ keep yr gear stashed in clear plastic boxes or wire trays (so u can c wots in em!) and it keeps everything neat on tha shelves and easier 2 get stuff up and down

☺ boxes can be stowed in other nifty places – like under tha bed

### tag it

☺ put big labels on all your drawers, files and boxes – it'll help u find stuff when u need it

**file it**

☺ if u have loads of paper stuff – homework, letters, doodles, etc – get a filing system sorted. Molly got an old filing cabinet from her mum's office & put a bunch of suspended files in it in abc order – it sorted her room no probs

☺ if you have a copy of something on computer ditch the paper version – it ain't necessary in this day & age! (always back-up yr stuff tho – in case yr computer breaks down!)

**stow it**

☺ if u have a small room, put stuff you don't need away until u do – eg, bag up your winter clothes in summer and bung em in the attic 4 a few months

**other stuff**

☺ shoe racks that hang from a rail keep mess off tha floor

☺ hooks on tha backs of doors give u xtra hanging space

☺ don't forget 2 use the "dead" space under beds & on tops of wardrobes

Now the groovy Missy's got us in the mood, any of you other Mates got some cheapo ways of adding boom! to your boudoir?

❝Accessories! Those little things that you don't actually *need* to exist but that can make your room great and a girl enjoys having around! Here's my essential guide...❞

# Princess's necessary accessories (for a better boudoir!)

**Beads** Add instant glamour by trimming lamps, curtains, cushions, and whatever else you can think of, with dingly-dangly bits and bobs.

**Clothes rail** Haven't you heard? Wardrobes are strictly for oldsters.

**Cushions** Give your room a soft romantic look, and provide plenty of comfy slouching opportunities for visiting mates, with as many cushions of different shapes sizes and materials as you can get hold of (see page 79 for cushion-making).

**Feathers** A bit of plumage is an inexpensive way of making your room look fabulously arty. Drape feather boas around mirrors and picture frames, and stick feathers into a vase instead of flowers – et voila, tres glam, mes amis!

**Glitter** Is something in your room looking sad, saggy and sort-of-dull? Glitterate it! There's really not much in this world that wouldn't look better with a coating of glitter paint lovingly slapped on it.

**Heavenly skies** Stick glow-in-the-dark stars on your ceiling, then simply lie back and visit a different universe.

**Joss sticks** Perfect for that new age chick vibe! And you don't even need to burn them to catch a whiff of their exotic scent.

**Knick-knacks** I like old perfume bottles; Molly has a thing for the stupidest joke shop products she can find; Bubble collects footballers' autographs (and has devoted a whole wall of her room to her fave team); Flower's room glistens with new age crystals (they're a source of healing power apparently); and Missy is mad about sunglasses (she currently owns 13 "bling-bling shades" – as she calls them). Whatever you're into, display it proudly in your room, it's what makes you *you*, and you different from the others!

**Lights** You can go from a cosy glowing den to a dazzling bright beauty salon with the flick of a switch. See if your mum's got a couple of old lamps you can jazz up, then try them in different places in your room to achieve the mood you want. For a magical touch, you can borrow the Christmas fairy lights and string them round your room. Coloured light bulbs can create a chilled-out glow and a mirror ball will give you an instant party atmosphere.

**Mirrors** Not only do mirrors make your room look bigger, but you get to catch glimpses of your beautiful self all the time – mmmwah mmmwah!! (That's the sound of you blowing kisses at your gorgeous reflection!) You can also use mirrors to reflect light around your room.

**Posters** OK, so putting up posters in your room is not an earth-shatteringly new idea, but how about getting creative with your poster displays, huh?!? My three best ideas for groovy postering:

**1** Be wacky: put your posters on the ceiling! Lie back on your bed and enjoy!

**2** Be cool: place your posters so they make a chequer-board design over one wall.

**3** Be arty: instead of just putting up ready-made posters, cut around your chosen footballer/pop star/kitten – their life-like shape will really make them stand out and add depth to your room (as we designer types like to say).

**Rugs** Are you bored with staring at the same old floor? Add a fresh look with a brightly coloured rug! (Also very useful for hiding stains from mum's beady eyes.)

**Smells** Want to make your mates think they've just stepped into an exotic, Eastern palace? Then get in a load of potpourri, scented candles, joss sticks, essential oils or incense. They won't even notice your room's a mess, just the gorgeous aromas!

**WATCH IT, Mate!** Burning stuff like incense, candles and essential oils can be a fire risk! Always ask Mum or Dad if you can use them, never leave anything that is burning unattended and make sure you always extinguish them properly.

That sure is some awesome accessorizing there, Princess!

**66** Thanks, Molly, I guess all I'm telling our Mate is that she should have fun, be herself and surround herself with lovely things! **99**

**66** Hey, now P's finished, isn't it time for my bit? **99**

Okey-dokey, Bubs! And now, proving she is handier than a handy man with a set of extra hands, it's the moment we've all been waiting for … Ms Handy-dandy herself, the one and only Bubble! (Cue, riotous applause and cheering!)

**66** I may not be the tidiest of the Mates or a trendy designer type like Princess, but 'cos my parents are obsessed by 'economizing' (yawnsville!) and my dad's a DIY nut, I've become something of a Handy Revamp Queen. **99**

71

## Funk up that junk (with Bubble!)

To begin doing up your old stuff and adding some magical touches to your room, all you need are some basic tools. See what you can cobble together from my list, then let your imagination go bananas!

## Useful stuff for beginner junk funkers

**Brushes, rollers, sponges, etc** Experiment with different ways of applying paint to get different effects and finishes.

**Day-glo paint** Ideal for creating glimmering stars and moons.

**Double-sided sticky tape** Great for when glue isn't fast enough!

**Dye** A messy, but brilliant way of giving old bedding, throws and curtains a new look. It's probably best to get your mum involved on this one, 'cos if she's anything like mine she'll go barmy if she catches you slopping great buckets of fuchsia dye around. (See page 91 for more tips.)

**Fun fur** Adds comfort, style and trendiness to any surface!

**Gemstones** Glue plastic ones on everything from mirrors to chair backs!

**Glue gun** Essential for sticking things to things!

**Glitter** Makes the world a happier place!

**Knobs** Give a yucky wardrobe, chest of drawers, or even your bedroom door a totally radical new image simply by replacing the handles.

**Metallic felt-tips** Great for drawing fancy patterns on to stuff.

**Muslin (or any floaty material)** Perfect for making cheap curtains and fancy bed canopies.

**Paint** Can't afford a big tin? No leftovers? Get your hands on some tester pots and use them to paint funky borders or murals or on woodwork and doors. Specialist paints are great. My current faves are denim finish, glitter paint, gold and silver metallic paints and hot pink in gloss. Look in your local DIY store for inspiration.

**Ribbon** Girly stuff up with bows.

**Silk flowers** Pretend you live in a sunny meadow and stick 'em over yer walls, drawers or wastebasket!

**Stencils** One of the grooviest tools in the junk funker's box of tricks! Use stencils to paint themes and patterns (people, flowers, angels, animals, etc) on to your stuff –

including using them with fabric paints on your cushions, duvet cover and curtains.

**Tassels** Use big chunky ones instead of drawer knobs or use them as classy curtain tie-backs!

**Trimmings** Get the glue gun out and add velvet, fringes, beads and braiding to *everything*!

**Velcro** Can't be bothered sewing? Stick this on with fabric glue, or get no-sew, iron-on hems.

❝Got your kit together? Fancy testing out your junk funker skills? C'mon, Mate, you sound up for one of my famous DIY projects!❞

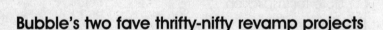

## Bubble's two fave thrifty-nifty revamp projects

**Project 1: Jazzing up an old wooden chair**
*What you need:*
★ Paint (gloss is best) ★ Brushes ★ Old newspaper ★ Sandpaper (maybe) ★ Oh, and an old chair!

### *What you do:*

Ask your parents for any leftover paint, then stand your chair on plenty of newspaper (to stop dreaded drips!) and paint as much of it as you can see. Wait for the paint to dry (a couple of hours or so), then turn the chair over and paint the other side. (If you are painting a varnished surface you may need to sandpaper it first otherwise the new paint won't stay on properly.)

**Other stuff:** Use your imagination to add personal touches to your revamped chair: how about sticking buttons or gemstones around the edges (not on the seat bit though, ouch!), painting your name on the back, stencilling it with lovehearts, or painting bits of it different colours for a rainbow effect?

**❝**If you have mismatched furniture you can paint it all the same colour so it looks like a set. White gloss is boss 'cos it's clean, bright, modern and goes with everything.**❞**

# Princess's Parent Persuader No 5

YOU WANT: your bedroom to be a parent-free zone while you and your mates do all the painting and stuff yourselves

THE PARENTS WANT: to be in charge of everything

TYPICAL PARENT QUOTE: "No, you'll only make a mess."

MINI WHEEDLE: Ask them to start you off by showing you how it's done but then ask them to let you get on with it, and perhaps agree that they are allowed to check your progress once an hour.

MAJOR WHEEDLE: Announce your intention to become an interior designer when you are older. Then say, however, you fear that unless you are given this opportunity to explore your ambitions, the fire that burns within your soul will be smothered for ever.

**Project 2: Beautifying a boring table-** knick-knacks and glitter.

*What you need:*

★ Paintbrush ★ Clear, quick-drying varnish ★ paint ★ Interesting knick-knacks you want to immortalize on your table-top. Pick things that will lie flat like photos, confetti, pressed leaves or flowers, cut-outs of angels, stars – or whatever else goes with your room's theme.

*What you do:*

Make sure the table-top is clean and dry then paint it with the glitter paint, if you've got it. You can also paint on a layer of varnish and sprinkle it with some glitter. Next, carefully brush the backs of your knick-knacks with varnish and lay them down flat on the table (they must be almost completely flat!). Once everything is in place, gently give your top a few more coatings of varnish. Leave each coat to dry for about 30 minutes, or according to the instructions on the label, before painting the next layer on. It will need about five coats in all.

**er stuff:** Now you've got the table-top looking great, what about painting the legs with glitter paint or gluing on plastic gemstones, sea shells or even plastic spiders!

❝I've got heaps of football stuff varnished on to mine – including posters of all the players from my fave team and a ticket stub from when Dad took me to see 'em. It looks top banana!❞

Feel inspired by Bubble's super-arty-crafty creativeness? Need some new gear for zero dosh? Want to add some very special features to your room? Look no further than our next thrilling chapter, Mate, where we will explore some splendiferous stuff to make. Onwards!

## Stuff to Make

Unless your parents are, like, trazillionaires and have hired you a small army of interior designers, there comes a time in every Mate's makeover where she will have to get seriously practical. So if you want to know how to do everything from making a cushion to painting a mural, read on! (Unless, that is, you actually WANT YOUR DAD TO GO AND GET HIS DIY MANUAL... Ha! I thought that would get your bum into gear!)

### Flower's Foolishly easy-to-make Cushions

66 Cushions are a simple way of making your room look inviting. Here are my basic cushion-making instructions – use them to make anything from pretty mini-cushions to whopping great floor cushions! And don't worry, you don't need to be a super seamstress to make them! 99

### *You will need:*

★ Material (Stuff like fun fur is easy to work with, and it's cheap and looks gorgeous. Or maybe you've got some old clothes you can cut up and use?)

★ Stuffing (For this, you could use an old cushion, foam pad, soft-toy stuffing, old clothes, tights, etc or polystyrene balls.)

★ Thread ★ Needle (longer, sturdier ones are sometimes easier to work with) ★ Pins ★ Scissors ★ Velcro or popper fasteners (optional)

### *What you do*:

**1** Decide what size you want your cushion to be. If you are using a loose filling this can be pretty flexible – but a 35 cm x 35 cm shape will give you a nice medium-sized cushion. If you are making a case for a foam pad or old cushion, you will need to measure it and add 1.5 cm on each side to allow for the seams.

**2** Cut out one cushion front and one back from your material, according to your chosen measurements.

**3** Place the two bits of material with the right sides facing together (ie, so the patterned sides are not showing), and pin it all the way around – this will keep the material in place. Then stitch round three sides

about 1.5 cm from the edge, leaving the [  ]
side open.

**4** Remove the pins and turn the cover [  ]
Insert your stuffing, then turn under the edges of the
opening by about 1.5 cm. Now stitch the Velcro or
poppers into place on the inside edge of the opening
or stitch it closed.

**5** Lie back on your lovely new cushion – you've earned
a rest!

**Special note:** If you are using loose filling, like polystyrene
balls, and want to be able to wash your cushion cover,
it will be easier if you put your filling into an inner cushion
case first. You can make it exactly as above only slightly
smaller (about a centimetre less on all sides), using
unwanted scraps of material
and stitching it closed.

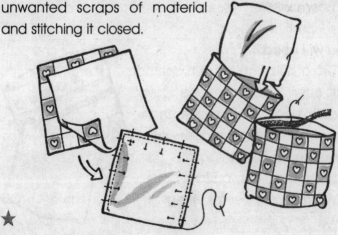

## The BMs secret stash stowaway cushion!

One of the great things about making your own
cushions is that you can customize them into the
perfect device for keeping precious private stuff (like
your diary) away from the prying eyes of irksome siblings
or nosy parents!

### *You will need:*

★ Two cushion covers with one side
left open on each (One cover
should be slightly smaller than
the other – only the bigger one
needs to be in nice fabric.)

★ Loose filling or two foam pads

★ Velcro or popper fastenings

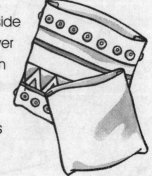

## What you do:

**1** Fold the opening on each cover inwards so that it has a hem of 2.5 cm all the way round. Attach the Velcro (using fabric glue) or stitch the poppers to the inner edges of the opening – so that when your cushion is closed everything is concealed and the sides all look the same.

**2** Stuff the smaller cover with your filling and simply insert your secret stash roughly in the middle. (If you're using the foam pads, they will act like a sandwich kinda thing.) Then close your cushion.

**3** Insert the smaller inner cushion upside-down (so that its opening is on the opposite side to the second opening) into the slightly bigger outer cushion and close that too.

**How it works:** The stowaway cushion looks normal but even if a snooper starts meddling with it, the cunning fastenings should put them off. However, if you possess supersnoopers for relatives, you should slip a "conscience-pricking notelet" inside the first cover. It should read something like this:

Dear Supersnooper,
Please immediately halt your snooping! If you go any further you will unearth my diary's little sanctuary. I've hidden it here for a reason, because it contains my private thoughts and feelings — if I'd meant for you to see them I wouldn't have hidden them. Please respect my rights as a human being. If you want to know something about me, you could always try talking to me.
Be warned: no good will come of further snooping.
Love, peace and harmony,

_____ (your name here)

**❝**Grrr! There's nothing as annoying as someone getting hold of your stuff. I should know, nothing I own is safe from the sticky paws of my little sis... That is until I made myself a pair of really natty pocket curtains – they're curtains but with loads of pockets all over them! It took ages for Sticky Paws to realize I was hiding things in my 'pockets'; and now, to be safe, I switch things around constantly or use the ones higher up.**❞**

## Bubble's (semi-secret) pocket curtains

### *You will need:*

★ Curtains – solid colour ones look better 'cos they show the pockets off, but you could use any ★ A bunch of old scarves, bandanas, napkins or back pockets ripped from bum of old jeans ★ Pins ★ Needle ★ Thread

### *What you do:*

**1** Turn each scarf (etc) into pockets of various shapes and sizes by either folding in half diagonally, so you have a triangular shape with one corner facing directly down, or folding in half to give you a rectangle shape.

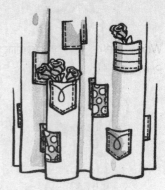

**2** Lay the curtains flat and pin on your pockets, either in rows or higgedly-piggedly.

**3** Now sew the pockets on to the curtains, leaving the top of each pocket open, and remove the pins as you go.

nice way 2 keep things tidy!

**"**You could have some silk flowers peeking out of each pocket for a hippy touch!**"**

Wow, we're really getting going with the nifty ideas –
Princess, how about you?

**❝**Well of course, being the most
*princessy* of us all, I think I should
probably be the one to tell our
Mate how to make her bed look fit
enough for royalty. Mates, be
prepared to be the envy of girls
everywhere as you learn to
make:**❞**

## Classic canopies and floaty four-posters ★

**❝**Use a simple canopy to highlight
your bed, or go for full-on fantasy
with the surprisingly easy-to-make
four-poster.**❞**

**WATCH IT,**
Mate!

Since this involves the rather tricky business of screwing
things into ceilings, it will be necessary to call upon the help
of at least one of your parents. (We know you want to do it
yourself, but think of it as doing them a favour – after all,
they like to feel needed.)

### *For a basic canopy, you will need:*

★ Lightweight floaty material (like muslin, netting, or something silky; and preferably one that doesn't fray or run – so you don't have to sew loads of boring hems)

★ 160 cm length of fishing line (also called monofilament)

★ Four biggish screw eyes (these have the bodies of screws, but instead of having flat, screw heads they have a loop which is used to hold wire or thread)

### *What you do:*

**1** Cut your material to the size you require. (For a single bed, your canopy should be slightly wider and longer than your bed – approximately 125 cm x 235 cm.)

**2** Attach a 40-cm length of the fishing line on to each corner of the canopy by sewing it on using a large-eyed darning needle – make about seven secure stitches then leave the end dangling.

CEILING

**3** Call upon parent to fix screws into the ceiling above your bed. They should be spaced apart to the exact measurements of your canopy.

**4** Ask a parent to help tie the dangly ends of the fishing line securely to the screw eye in the ceiling. Your canopy should now look as though it is hovering above your bed!

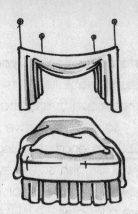

**To make the four-poster version, you will also need:**
★ Four lengths of your material (approx 20 cm x 2.65 m) for the corner drop panels

**What you do:**

**Follow 1 as above**

**2** Fabric glue or sew each of the drop panels on to the canopy top. Make sure the top of each drop panel fits squarely around each corner of the canopy top.

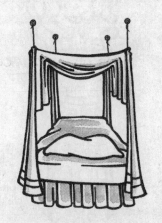

**Follow 2, 3 and 4 above**

Then stand in amazement, as you behold your four lovely drop panels cascading beautifully down to the floor!

**Last step (optional):** For an added touch of sumptuous lushness, tie each panel with a ribbon or scarf halfway down.

❝Jazz up your canopy by painting on a design of your choice. Try doing stars using gold fabric paint or a quote written in fancy lettering ("sleep perchance to dream..." from Mr W Shakespeare, for example).❞

❝Don't forget you could give your canopy a crazy dose of colour by tie-dyeing it! Anything that stays still for more than five mins in our house gets shoved in the tie-dye bucket, we're mad for it! It's a great way to turn dull things into multicoloured masterpieces! Here's how we do it round our way:❞

# How to tie-dye with Flower power!

**You will need:**

★ The object to be dyed (old cotton sheets and pillowcases are perfect) ★ Dye ★ Rubber gloves ★ Elastic bands ★ Salt ★ Two old buckets or bowls ★ Cold water

**What you do:**

**1** Start by pinching bits of the material into cone shapes and tightly wrapping them with the elastic bands. This gives you swirly circular patterns when you've finished – the bigger the cone the bigger the circle will be.

**2** Following the manufacturer's instructions on the package, carefully mix the dye with water in the bowl or bucket.

**3** Sprinkle a few teaspoons of salt into the dye mixture – this will help set the pigment in the dye.

**4** Then, wearing your rubber gloves to stop your hands staining, carefully dunk your object-to-be-dyed into the dye and leave it to soak for about an hour.

**5** Carefully remove your object from the dye into an old bowl, let it sit and dry for about 3–4 hours. Then rinse thoroughly with water and remove the elastic bands. Hey presto, groovy bedding/wall-hanging/curtains *and* a piece of original artwork made by you!

WATCH IT, Mate!

Dyeing can be a messy business. Always make sure you've protected all surfaces with heaps of newspapers and wear old clothes. And you'd better ask The Parents' permission before you turn your house into a rainbow land of splishy splashy loveliness (they might not see it that way).

Speaking of rainbows and splishy splashy effects reminds me of Bubble with a paint brush!

**❝**OK, so I may be a bit messy, but that's the price you pay for creativity! I'm sure I could show our Mate some interesting paint effects for her walls.**❞**

Go on then.

# Splish-splash: a lesson in paint effects by Mistress Bubble

❝Nothing transforms a room quite as dramatically as painting it. Here, I've picked out the most dramatic techniques I've come across for painting your walls.❞

## Candy-stripe walls

You can do this on just one wall or a small area. If you're after a classy look use subtle shades or if you fancy a bit of an eye-ball battering use bolder, contrasting colours. Guess which one I like best?!

### You will need:

★ Two shades of paint ★ Painter's tape ★ Plumb line (You'll probably have to agree to a parent helping you on this one.) ★ Smallish paint brush

### What you do:

1 Paint your wall using one of the colours and let it dry (bearing in mind that some paints might need a second coat).

**2** Mark off your stripes, by blocking out every other 15-cm vertical section using the tape. The plumb line (basically a string with a weight at the bottom) will help you keep your tape straight 'cos when you hold it at the top of the wall the weight at the bottom keeps the string taut and exactly straight.

**3** Carefully paint the exposed area of wall with your second colour, leave to dry, then remove tape (it's designed not to rip paint off walls).

WATCH IT, Mate!

Mind the mess by putting down loads of newspaper or old sheets over *everything* not to be painted before you start. Mark off the surface to be painted using painter's tape to stop paint splishing into adjoining areas. And make sure the room is ventilated or the fumes will get you!

## Murals

Even if you think you have, like, zero artistic skills, painting an effective mural can be surprisingly easy. Try these two:

### Tropical scene mural
*You will need:*

★ A few tester pots of paints (in brown, green, yellow and blue) ★ Paint brush

## What you do:

**1** For the sand, paint a bit of yellow on the bottom of your wall. (You could even add a bit of real sand to the paint for genuine texture effect!)

**2** Paint a long brown trunk coming out of the sand. Start the trunk broad at the bottom and taper it at the top.

**3** Add a few spiky, green, palm type leaves. Simple, eh?

## Mega-massive mural

The trouble with doing bigger, more ambitious murals is that it can be tricky keeping the proportions right when you draw things on a large scale – but not when you try this method!

### You will need:

★ Pencil ★ Rubber ★ Sketch pad ★ Ruler ★ Measuring tape ★ Paint ★ Brushes and a big dollop of courage!

### What you do:

**1** Start off by making a sketch of your design on paper. Then draw a grid over your drawing, so you end up with, say, lots of 5 cm x 5 cm boxes.

**2** Draw a corresponding grid in pencil on your wall but at four times the scale (with 20 cm x 20 cm boxes).

**3** Now draw your design on the wall, being careful to copy into the larger boxes only what's in the corresponding smaller boxes from your sketch. Once you're happy with your drawing, you can get going with the paint.

> **Best Mates TOP TIP**
>
> If you're not allowed to paint your walls, try decorating them with inspirational quotes! If you hear or read something brilliant, all you do is copy it out on a piece of paper (I like to do mine on the computer and use fancy lettering) and hang it where you can see it. My current inspirational quote is: "Don't let school interfere with your education!" (said by famous American author Mark Twain).

Well, BMs, I'm sure our Mate is suffering from information overload right about now! I think it's time to see what bothersome bedroom worries still remain unsolved in Matesville. BMs, get your problem-solving advice ready!

# Your Bedroom-Blitzing Problems Sorted

Can't decide between funky futuristic and junky retro? Having difficulties sharing your room with your pesky sis? Is living in a "shoe box" getting you down? We've been there! And now we're here to help you! Fire away, readers!

**letter 1**

### Babyish room gloom

Dear Best Mates

The decor of my bedroom hasn't changed since I was six! Although I like pink, everything I've got is pink – including a stencilled-on border of pink baby rabbits. What's the easiest way of giving it an older look?

Ex-bunny lover, 10, Liverpool

**What the Best Mates say**

 What about painting all your walls halfway up with a new colour leaving the pink on the top half! Now that's cool!

 Then you could get a trendy wallpaper border to cover up your bunnies.

 Yeah, pick a border that matches the pink and your new colour to tie it all in. I like pink and purple together, then maybe a pink, purple and orange striped border.

limit the number of stuffed toys u have out – maybe keep yr 5 faves then store the rest away

## letter 2

**Poster poser**

Dear Best Mates

I would love to cover one of my walls with posters of my fave band, but my mum and dad say I can't because posters will "ruin the walls". Please help, I can't stand my dull walls any longer!

Florence, 11, Wolverhampton

### What the Best Mates say

 Invest in a packet of Blu-tack, or similar, then invite your parents to a demonstration in your room of its non-marking qualities! Also try offering them a guarantee, promising to repaint your walls if they do get damaged (but in bright pink, ha!).

Explain, with a sulky pout, that they are suffocating your artistic spirit. Modern parents hate being accused of this, and will hopefully feel bad and give in to your not unreasonable demands!

## letter 3

**Little room = big problem!**

Dear Best Mates

Please help me, I have the smallest bedroom known to girlkind – we're talking seriously shoe box. Got any tips?

Billie-Mae, 9, a wee den somewhere

### What the Best Mates say

 OK, Mate, anything to help. Here's a Blitzer Bitz special just for you!

## ★ Blitzer bitz! ★

***What to do if your room is small (besides weep and stomp your foot!)***

★ Get in loads of mirrors – they make a room look bigger and brighter

★ Avoid patterns and dark colours – they'll make it seem cramped and "busy".

★ Go for light colours and leave your ceiling white (dark colours make ceilings appear lower, light colours appear to heighten them).

★ Avoid unnecessary furniture – for example, have shelves instead of bookcases

★ Get rid of your clutter!

★ Beg your parents to put in the ultimate space-saving device, an alcove bed – the groovy ones with the bed on a raised platform with a desk and storage space (and sometimes even a sofa below).

★ If The Parents won't go for the above, you could always try making your bed look sofa-like when you've got friends round. Simply push your bed lengthways against a wall, remove your pillow, cover all of the bed with your duvet or a throw and line up a row of pillows against the wall.

## letter 4

### New curtains for certain!

Dear Best Mates

My room's done in a moon and stars theme and I've found this wonderful piece of material with all the signs of the zodiac on which I'm desperate to have as new curtains for my room. The trouble is, I haven't got a clue how to make curtains, I can't sew, and my mum says she hasn't got time to make some. Any ideas?

Kelly, 11, Ipswich

## What the Best Mates say

u can make curtains out of anything without needing to sew! try pinning the material straight on 2 the top of the window frame – and use a scarf or ribbon tied round the middle of the material when u want 2 let some light in! better ask the parents' permission b4 u do this 1 though

▶

Or for an instant proper curtain, you could turn over a hem of about 15 cm at the top of your material and fix it down using some of that no-sew iron-on hem stuff. This would leave you a channel all along the top of your "curtains" which you could slot a net curtain rod or curtain pole through – which could then be hung as normal. You might want to use iron-on hems for the sides and bottoms of your curtains to prevent fraying.

## Bedroom-sharing horror!

Dear Best Mates

My seven-year-old sister Daisy has had to move into my room after my mum had our new baby brother a few months ago. I am in despair! What used to be my big, beautiful boudoir has become a pig-sty of broken doll-parts, teddies and odd socks, and just this week the wall sprouted a crop of tacky Cinderella posters. Daisy is really beginning to annoy me – I just have no privacy left. What can I do?

Cindy, 10, West Dorset

### What the Best Mates say

What about poor Daisy?! She's used to being the youngest, now she's been "replaced" by a baby. She's totally lost her room and to finish it all off her big sister is annoyed with her! Try and find it in your heart to welcome her into your room.

Yeah, well that's OK for you to say, Flower. You don't have to put up with the hours of screechy, off-key recorder practise or the endless threats to "tell Mum on you" like me and Cindy here do.

I think you've got to gently set some limits. What about dividing the room in two and getting her to keep all her stuff confined to her bit. And as you're the oldest and probably have more stuff, maybe you should negotiate the bigger half! Colour-coding would be a good way of marking where the room's divided; see if your parents will let you paint your half of the room in a different colour to Daisy's.

▶

For a bit of privacy, you could have a four-poster canopy over your bed (see page 87), and maybe even have it curtained all the way round – then make it a rule that Daisy isn't allowed in your "tent"!

## letter 6

**Day-glo no go, says Mum**

Dear Best Mates
I really want to paint my walls bright orange, but my mum says absolutely no way. How can I persuade her to change her mind?

Ella, 9, South London

x

Go for both! Paint your walls then put up little wallpaper borders around the top or halfway up. You can get some designer-looking ones with trendy geometric patterns and they are easy to put up and take down.

## letter 8

**My dull room hell**
Dear Best Mates
Everything in my room is very plain; I have a grey carpet, beige curtains, cream-coloured walls, and a matching bedside table, dresser and wardrobe in a boring oak colour. What are the cheapest and easiest ways of injecting some life into my dull room?

Lily, 11, Bleaksville

## What the Best Mates say

 You're in need of some kitschy colour – fast! First, buy a small can of paint, say in pink, and carefully paint pink squares of different sizes all over your walls. Next, buy some matching pink tissue paper, enough to cover your window. Then, cut out loads of different-sized square "peepholes" into the tissue paper. Make a cardboard frame the same size as your window frame and stick the tissue paper to it. Stick the whole thing to the window frame with Blu-tack. Finally, lay down a pink rug (shaggy bath mats look cute and are usually cheaper than ordinary rugs). Ta-daa! Within a few hours your room will look very trendy and modern!

 I'd cover up some of that wood as well – a pretty scarf thrown over the bedside table would make all the difference.

u need 2 give yr room something new every week – even a different screensaver on yr computer or a new poster of your fave celeb – new stuff keeps it looking fresh!

### Funky or Junky?

Dear Best Mates

I'm about to completely blitz my bedroom! The trouble is I'm torn between two great themes: funky futuristic (lots of silver and plastic, and things with aliens on) or junky, 1970s retro (with lots of crazy geometric patterns and a groovy orange and brown colour scheme). What do you think?

Marina Muddlehead, 10, Manchester

## What the Best Mates say

 I think you should do the quiz in the next thrilling chapter!

# The Quiz

This is the bit where we find out exactly what bedroom theme would *really* suit your personality, just how much natural style you truly possess and whether you're a Handy Annie or a Dotty Disaster of home improvement. Yes, Mates, it's the ultimate bedroom-based quiz...

## R U a boudoir beauty or a bedroom banana?

Tick one of the answers after each question, then turn to page 111, add up your scores and find your profile. And please note, we only accept honest answers here, Mate!

**1 Pick your favourite bedroom colour scheme from the following:**
**a)** Bright white with the odd glint of gold
**b)** Sumptuous feast of reds
**c)** Pale green and cotton-candy pink
**d)** Citrusy lemon with a blackcurrant purple contrast
**e)** Burnt orange rippled with azure blue
**f)** Oatmeal blended with beige blotches

**2 Which of these "design features" would/does most make you cringe around your house?**

**a)** Net curtains – sooo frumpy!

**b)** Flowery chintzy furniture in the front room – enough said!

**c)** So-called "ambient" lighting – what's that about?!

**d)** Brass pokers set by the *gas* fire – they don't fool anyone!

**e)** Designer shoe tidies – how posey and fiddly!

**f)** Reading matter in the toilet – yuck! I don't want to think about what goes on in there, thanks!

**3 The last arty-crafty thing you did was (tick whichever is closest):**

**a)** Helped Dad put up some shelving

**b)** Put some beads in my hair

**c)** Had a look at one of Mum's interior design magazines!

**d)** Jazzed up a couple of boxes to use as storage

**e)** Made a cotton-wool snowman when I was five

**f)** Customized a postcard to use as a bookmark (well, OK, I wrote my name on it in glitter pen!)

**4 Which of the following places would you most like to visit?**

**a)** Sunny California – you get to wear groovy hipster flares, little crop tops and ride around the awesome countryside on the back of a huge motorbike, your long hair flowing in the warm breeze

**b)** Africa on safari – nothing could be better than being camped out under the stars listening to the strange sounds of the sub-Saharan night

**c)** Roswell in New Mexico – it's where all the space aliens land apparently. Now that would be a great science project...

**d)** Rome – it's meant to be really chic and stylish, plus all that architecture and art must be so inspiring

**e)** New York City – a dead-cool city full of fascinating people... it would be so cool to just hang out people-watching at a "sidewalk" cafe

**f)** The Great Barrier Reef in Australia – snorkelling in crystal clear water among the amazing coral and colourful fishes (avoiding the big ones with teeth though!)

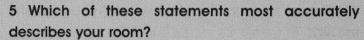

**5 Which of these statements most accurately describes your room?**

**a)** Matching duvet, curtains and lampshade (bought by Mum), muted colour scheme

**b)** Cosy and welcoming, with lots of knick-knacks and cute details

**c)** Very modern, with everything in its right place, bold and bright colour scheme

**d)** Colourful and curious, with loads of quirky objects

**e)** Quite moody, packed with interesting textures, photos and dim lighting

**f)** Stylish – with co-ordinated fabrics, girly touches and a cool, light colour scheme

**6 Which of these statements most accurately reflects the state of your bedroom? (Come on, be honest now – go and have a quick look!)**

**a)** OK I admit it I'm a tidy freak – everything's very ordered, I even line up the gonks on my desk in size order

**b)** I don't see the point of fussing about making places look fancy – and you won't find a load of unnecessary possessions either, just my books and bed kept in an orderly fashion

**c)** It smells lovely (I wafted some room scent around earlier) and my friends tell me it looks "casually elegant"

**d)** The floor is pretty much covered with stuff and there's a dust ball bigger than the cat lurking under the bed

**e)** A bit ramshackle, with the odd heap of clothes and books here and there – and, oops, a couple of days' worth of cups which Mum keeps asking me to bring downstairs

**f)** It's been a couple of days since it had a good tidy but I always like to have things cleared away and the bed made

**7 How often would you say you experiment with a different personal look? (Pick nearest statement.)**

**a)** My look is perfectly fine, I hate all that fashionable stuff – only the other day the headmistress praised my no-nonsense uniform

**b)** I love shopping for new clothes and shoes

**c)** I like to muck about with hair accessories and little bits of make-up and nail varnish

**d)** I have two looks – daytime and night-time!

**e)** I like to customize my clothes to my taste – I think I look individual (although Mum says "scruffy"!)

**f)** I always try on loads of outfits before I go out and I just recently had a new hairstyle

**8 Your desk suddenly becomes wobbly, what do you do?**

**a)** Get excited about your new "project" and ask Dad if you can borrow his saw

**b)** Tell your parents you need a new one

**c)** Stick a bit of cardboard under the wonky leg to stop it wobbling

**d)** Ask a parent to fix it

**e)** Do your homework sitting on your bed instead

**f)** Keep meaning to look at it, then forget

**9 If you could become one of the following, which career would you choose?**

**a)** Fitness guru to the famous

**b)** Pop star

**c)** Ecologist

**d)** Interior designer

**e)** Science teacher

**f)** Writer

**10 Which of the following would you most like to have in your bedroom? (They all cost the same!)**

**a)** A chic fitted wardrobe in pale wood and shiny chrome

**b)** The latest high-tech music system

**c)** An amazing four-poster bed canopy made of Japanese silk

**d)** A laptop computer with Internet access

**e)** An alcove bed – the kind with a raised bunk on top and a swinging sofa underneath

**f)** Double-glazing – allowing peace and quiet for homework completion

Now find out what kind of bedroom blitzer you are!

| | | | | | | |
|---|---|---|---|---|---|---|
| **Question 1** | a = 1 | b = 4 | c = 3 | d = 5 | e = 2 | f = 6 |
| **Question 2** | a = 3 | b = 1 | c = 6 | d = 2 | e = 5 | f = 4 |
| **Question 3** | a = 5 | b = 3 | c = 1 | d = 2 | e = 6 | f = 4 |
| **Question 4** | a = 3 | b = 5 | c = 6 | d = 1 | e = 4 | f = 2 |
| **Question 5** | a = 6 | b = 3 | c = 2 | d = 5 | e = 4 | f = 1 |
| **Question 6** | a = 2 | b = 6 | c = 1 | d = 5 | e = 4 | f = 3 |
| **Question 7** | a = 10! | b = 2 | c = 3 | d = 5 | e = 4 | f = 1 |
| **Question 8** | a = 5 | b = 1 | c = 2 | d = 3 | e = 6 | f = 4 |
| **Question 9** | a = 5 | b = 2 | c = 3 | d = 1 | e = 6 | f = 4 |
| **Question 10** | a = 1 | b = 2 | c = 3 | d = 4 | e = 5 | f = 6 |

## If you scored under 18 you are a: Boudoir beauty!

**Ups:** Wow, are you classy or what?! You instinctively know what's stylish and aren't afraid to experiment with adventurous new looks – you are a trendsetter and everyone secretly wants to be just like you.

**Downs:** You can be a bit snobby about other people's tastes, and don't actually like doing DIY that much – after all you might spoil your manicure!

**You are most like:** Princess

**You should try:** Princess's four-poster canopy (page 87)

## If you scored 18–25 you are a: Slumber-pad perfectionist!

**Ups:** Can there be anybody slicker than you? We think not! You really enjoy experimenting with different looks, are amazingly organized and practical and are fashion-aware without being faddy.

**Downs:** You are a bit ruthless sometimes, old stuff can be put to good use too, y'know. And when was the last time you hugged teddy, huh? Whaddya mean, he's in storage?! Tut!

**You are most like:** Missy

**You should try:** Missy's cool storage ideas (page 64)

## If you scored 26–33 you are a: Cosy-den darling!

**Ups:** You are a very spiritual, emotional kinda girl and really respect the environment (including that of your bedroom!), which is reflected in the tranquil vibes coming from you and your homely nest.

**Downs:** Sometimes your taste can get a bit *too* girly and cute – you could try to be just a little bit more adventurous.

**You are most like:** Flower
**You should try:** revamping an old tabl...

## If you scored 34–41 you are a: Beach bohemian

**Ups:** You have a very individual sense of style – some would say kooky. Everybody loves coming round to yours, not just 'cos you are a great hostess, but 'cos every so often there's a new weird and wonderful creation to look at.

**Downs:** More tidying and less deep-thinking could see you reach Boudoir Beauty status – but then you wouldn't be lovely you!

**are most like:** Molly

**You should try:** decluttering your room the feng shui way (page 63)

## If you scored 42–50 you are a: Bunk punk!

**Ups:** Everybody thinks you haven't got a clue when it comes to style – but actually you've got the most style of the lot! It's just that you are a deeply eccentric, troubled genius, and others are too conventional to see it! Plus you are amazingly practical.

**Downs:** The chaos! The reason nobody understands your sensational style is because everyone is too horrified by the avalanche of muddy boots, grimy socks, books, paintings from when you were two, chocolate wrappers, stringless tennis rackets, and possibly a sleeping elephant or two, that greets them when your bedroom door is opened.

**You are most like:** Bubble

**You should try:** a mega mural (page 95)

## If you scored over 50 you are a: Bedroom banana!

**Ups:** You probably don't actually care you're a banana, 'cos you really can't be bothered with anything as earthly as style! You're probably busy pondering your science homework or something.

**Downs:** You're missing out on the joy of colour and other things of eye-pleasing loveliness!

**You are most like:** a banana!

**You should try:** to get out more!

## Almost goodbye!

Yes, it's getting near the time when we must leave you to get on with your Bedroom Blitz by yourself! Sob! But before we go, it occurred to us Best Mates that there's a ton of other thrilling themes we haven't even mentioned! So, lovers of prancing pink hippos, read on for more theme-related merriment.

# Other Room Revamps

First of all, let me start this chapter with an apology:

Dear lovers of the prancing pink hippo theme,
I regret that for reasons of good taste we are
unable to bring you coverage of this theme — there
really is only room for the best themed bedroom
ideas in this book!
Love,
The Best Mates xxx

OK, Mates, let's go through our most brilliant theme
ideas and our toppest tips to go with them!

## The BMs top 10 fave bedroom themes 'n' styles (in alphabetical order!)

### 1 American retro

Cool, clean 1950s look using lots of lime green and pale pink. Think old-fashioned jukeboxes, polka-dot prints and vintage Mickey Mouse posters.

Save your old Coke bottles and display them in a line with a silk flower popping out of each one.

Do one wall using the candy-stripe painting method described on page 93, using lime green and pale pink – it will look boss!

### 2 Arabian night-nights

Achieve this look with rich colours, exotic silky and satiny materials and a floaty canopy bed (see page 87). Try to give your room a tent-like feel by putting up swathes of material draped artly around. Think big decorative tassles, gold-framed mirrors and stick plastic gemstones everywhere.

**Thrifty TIP**

See if your mum's got any old party dresses in fab material that she'll let you cut up and use to make cushions – see how on page 79.

**Flash TIP**

Do a mural of a desert night sky on one wall! All you have to do is paint it a lovely dark midnight blue, then paint a huge bright full moon quite low down on the horizon and as many twinkly stars as you fancy.

## 3 Fashion passion

Make your room a trendy den with lots of fashion-inspired stuff. Go for a "boutique" look with loads of mirrors, a dressing table packed with interesting hair accessories and stuff to mess around with, and hang large floppy hats and slogan T-shirts on coat hangers around your walls.

**Thrifty TIP**

Put up lots of posters of fashion shoots cut from glossy magazines.

**Flash TIP**

For the colour scheme, go for bold, bright walls – one yellow, one orange and one red – leaving the last one white. Hey, you might need it as background for a "photo shoot"!

## 4 Hawaiian holiday

Go on a tropical vacation every day with this look! Establish your beachy atmosphere by painting the bottom half of your walls in sand-coloured textured paint

and the top halves in sea blue and add a palm mural. Accessorize with lots of exotic plastic flowers, cacti, etc and it's "Aloha, baby!"

**Thrifty TIP** Make a collage of photos of you and your family on holiday – also ask your friends to contribute snaps of themselves in beachwear!

**Flash TIP** Bamboo blinds would be, er, blinding!

**"**You'd better take a look at my parent-wheedling tactics on page 18 if you're after some of those though!**"**

## 5 Madame Mexico

Turn your dark dank pit into a scene of sizzling spiciness, with a hot orange and intense red colour scheme, then accessorize with chilli fairy lights and green plastic cacti.

Make a mini poncho for your teddy out of an old piece of material cut into an oblong shape, then make a slit in the middle for the head hole. Sooo cute!

Paint "flames" along the bottom borders of your walls using upward "swooshes" of alternate yellow, orange and red paint, then carefully outline them in black – hey, presto! A snazzy flame border!

## 6 Movie madness

Go for either a general glam celeb style or give your room a theme based on your favourite movie! Put film posters up on your wall, and fill your room with star-shaped stuff.

**Thrifty TIP** For a laugh, make a shrine to your fave film star by making a stand-up silhouette of them. (Cut around a pic of them from a mag and mount it on to cardboard.) Then stand your celeb on an altar (OK, your dressing table), surround it with candles and present them with regular "offerings" – like a piece of your choc!

 **Flash TIP** Stars' make-up tables always have lights around the mirrors – do the same with your bedroom mirror by stringing fairy lights around the edge! Now you can see just how gorgeous you really are – you star of the future you!

## 7 Pretty 'n' pink

Rejoice in being of the female species by unashamedly turning your boudoir into a girly, fluffy pink nest! Soften the pink with lots of creamy colours, and use lots of love-hearts and roses to add depth and delight!

 **Thrifty TIP** Make your room smell pretty as well as look pretty with a bowl of rosy or peachy potpourri

 **Flash TIP** For ultimate girly lounging, get a chaise longue. (Y'know one of those old-fashioned sofa things that looks like a cross between a mini-bed and a reclining chair.) You can make your own version of one by getting a sun lounger (if The Parents haven't got one to lend you, perhaps you could wheedle one?) and covering it with a 2-metre length of glossy pink imitation satin and lots of matching cushions.

## 8 Super sci-fi

Midnight blue walls, gold stars and arty murals (see page 95) of star-sign constellations would start this look off! Then think spaceships, aliens and any other futuristic stuff.

 Paint big almond-shaped alien eyes around your room in glow-in-the-dark paint – sp-sp-sp-spooky!

 Turn your bed into a hovering spaceship by copying the tips for the magical "flying" snooze-palace from page 45, but give your bed a space-age headboard and a silvery-grey duvet cover instead.

## 9 Two-for-one!

Can't decide between two themes? Have it all by using stuff from both – think futuristic witch or a hippy beach holiday! A good trick is to make your stuff reversible – or as much of it as you can!

**Thrifty TIP**

Make a two-themed cushion by having tiger-stripe fun fur on one side (jungle theme) and pink satin on the other (girly theme).

**Flash TIP**

Go totally bonkers and divide your room in two and have different themes on the two sides!

## 10 Urban honey

Get the look with minimum junk, modern furniture, graffiti doodles, and glossy ads of cool trainers used as posters.

Paint one wall with blackboard paint and stock up on chalk for mad doodle parties!

Leave a skateboard lying casually around for instant street cred. Don't worry, you don't actually need to know how to ride it; just squat low and park your bum on it, rocking it from side to side every now and again. People will think you're just a very modest, laid-back skate chick!

## And now, it really is "goodnight" from us…

And so, with a big sad sigh, we Best Mates must say night-night and sweet bedroom dreams to you, our newest Mate … but only for now! 'Cos we've got loads more to tell you about some other time.

See you soon,

Big hugs, and let the bedroom bug bite!

Molly
x

L8r Missy ☺

Just remember, accessorize,
accessorize, accessorize!
Princess xx

Peace, love and
a happy space
Flower xxxx

And, hey, hope your dream boudoir
comes true! Bubble! ooo